Buenas Noches
El Paso

Written by
Luke Lowenfield

Illustrated by
Hal Marcus

Buenas Noches El Paso
First Edition, 2019

Text © by Luke Lowenfield, 2019 • Lowenfield.com
Artwork © by Hal Marcus, 2019 • HalMarcus.com
Design by Jud Burgess / Substance • JudBurgess.com

Published by Paso al Sol
1319 N. Oregon
El Paso, TX 79902
(915) 920-8133
halmarcus123@gmail.com

No part of this publication may be reproduced in any form without prior written permission from the author and illustrator.

Library of Congress Cataloguing-in-Publication Data is on file.

ISBN # 978-0-578-55822-6

Printed in PRC

A very special thanks to the Junior League of El Paso for their community support.

Hal Marcus Gallery
1308 N. Oregon
El Paso, Texas 79902
(915) 533-9090
halmarcus.com

El Paso Strong

This book is dedicated to the
Moms and Dads, Abuelas y Abuelos,
and all the others who brighten the future
by reading with kids.

White-winged doves fly over me,
   searching for their nest,

And sing their sleepy evening song
   when it's time to rest.

   coo coo cachoo   coo coo cachoo

Buenas tardes, El Paso

When darkness cools the mountain down,
the star turns on each night.

It's like a big electric tattoo
made of dazzling light.

We talk inside while we cook.
Chiles sizzle and pop.

Our funny pets circle our legs
and wait for food to drop.

Buenas noches, El Paso

After my bath, I brush my teeth and look into the mirror.
The Rio outside reflects the moon and brings the nightlight nearer.

Cookie, my dog,
   lies with me to snuggle up in bed.

Mom and Dad rub my back
   then kiss me on the head.

Dulces sueños, El Paso

I dream of riding a mountain lion over the peaks and even higher.

I dream of backyard desert plants
bursting with flowers like fire.

I dream of climbing patio walls
with lizards and geckos for fun.

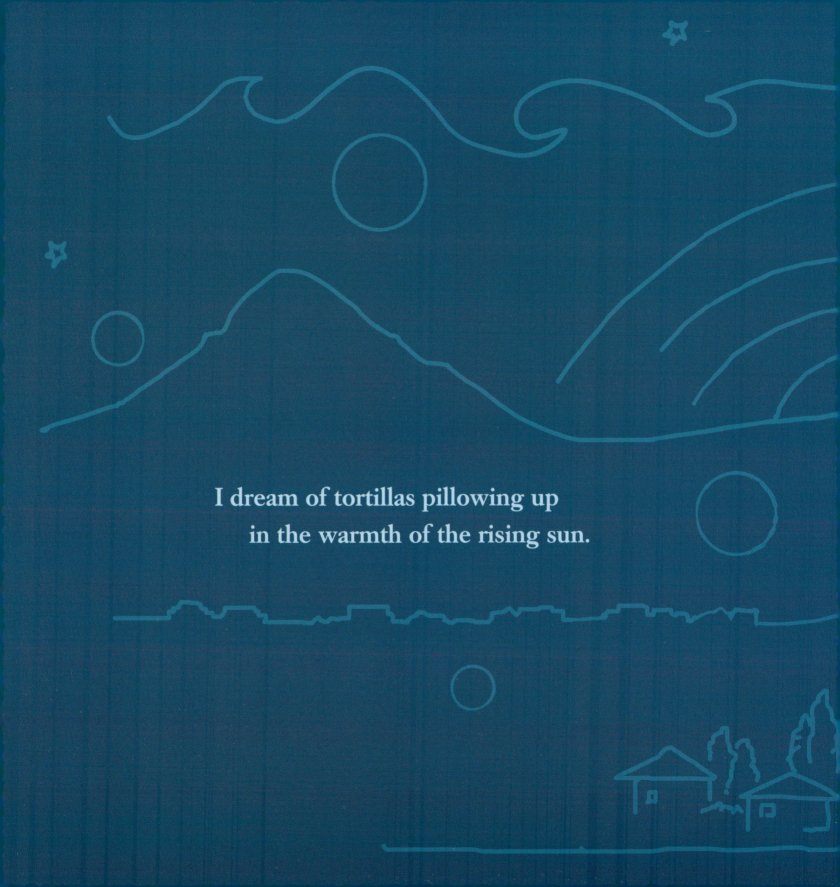
I dream of tortillas pillowing up
in the warmth of the rising sun.

My dreams become quiet,
    and I open my eyes to find another day.

The doves outside wake up, too,
    and start to fly away.

Luke Lowenfield is a writer born and raised in El Paso, Texas. His kids, Parker and Jackson, inspire him to see the world with the wonder and to write poetry and children's books that highlight the beauty around us all. Luke's stories encourage children to embrace their individuality and invite adults to remember the pure life they experienced when they were seeing everything for the first time.

He studied Children's Literature at Pennsylvania State University, and he's proud to publish his first book, *Buenas Noches El Paso*, to celebrate his hometown. Luke's mom, Rhonda, read stories to her four sons every night, which sparked a lifelong passion for reading and creative expression. He is especially grateful for his wife, Stacey, and the unconditional love she gives him.

El Paso painter Hal Marcus has been a professional artist for 50 years. He is a gallery owner, art collector, and publisher. His art work is best known for depicting El Paso's unique borderland culture, and it has been exhibited in museums and private collections worldwide.

He and his wife, Patricia, live in the historic Sunset Heights neighborhood in a 100-year-old home. Across the street is the Hal Marcus Gallery, which was established in 1996 and represents hundreds of local artists. Marcus has three children, Leilainia, Marco, and Adelaide; they are all artists living in California.

In 1976, Marcus founded Paso al Sol to publish fine art prints, cards, calendars and books. *Buenas Noches El Paso* is his eighth book and his third children's book.

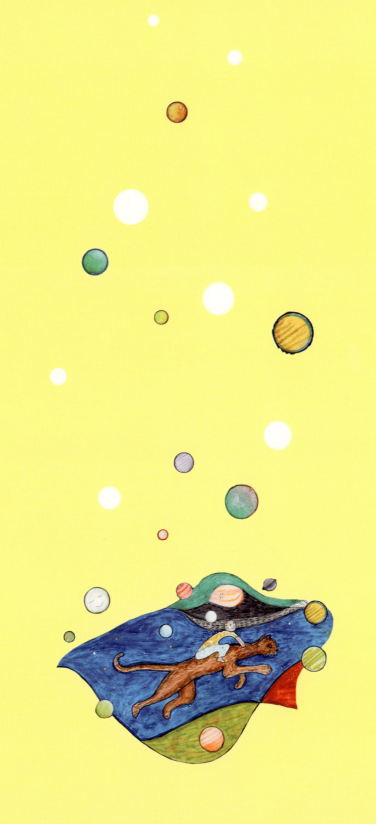